Where I'm Comin' From

~ Jay Walker ~

Where I'm Coming From. Copyright © 2018 Jay Walker. Produced and printed by Stillwater River Publications. All rights reserved. Written and produced in the United States of America. This book may not be reproduced or sold in any form without the expressed, written permission of the author and publisher.

Visit our website at www.StillwaterPress.com for more information.

First Stillwater River Publications Edition

ISBN-13: 978-1-946-30094-2
ISBN-10: 1-946-30094-2

1 2 3 4 5 6 7 8 9

Written by Jay Walker
Cover design by Kody Lavature
Published by Stillwater River Publications, Pawtucket, RI, USA.

The views and opinions expressed in this book are solely those of the author and do not necessarily reflect the views and opinions of the publisher.

Dedicated to Maureen Duggan Santos, Mark Colozzi, David Burr & all the teachers that stay with us long after graduation (or reasonable facsimile therein).

Table of Contents

The Gardener	7
Foreplay on Words	9
Close Analysis	13
Where I'm Comin' From	16
O Brother, Where Art Thou?	19
Change Now like Never Before	21
That Guy in That Picture	25
All of You	29
Changing Seasons	31
House Fire	33
A Little Sick [with apologies to Taylor Mali]	39
Cat & Mouse	42
Hurricane Nici	45
Sexual	47
Farewell to Fairy Fantasy	49
Grow Up	51
Blue	53
These Old Papers	54
Tattooed	57
So What?	60
Your Name in My Mouth	63
Color Blind	65
Education & Experience	69
The Good Fight	74
Junkie	76
A Haiku Series for a Series of Women	83
Words for Luke	87
More Random Haiku & Senryū	92
Time Now & Again [for Lois & Steve]	94

The Gardener

I could be an
          acrolinguist
     a word gymnast
deft at death-defying double tongue-flips
flying through your ear
    with the greatest of trap-ease
flex my trap & reach
    for the text trapeze
make it look easy to twirl turns of phrase on tongue
tease & amaze
    in a tale-spinning of the world on my trapezius
        spinning a yarn of yesterday
        spinning a web to trap you easily
     with feats of amazing athloquacity
            texterity
              & stanzamina enough
    to make even a thesaurus need to
        stop
          catch its breath
            & still only come up with
                  "Damn."
I *could* do that
    but I'm afraid of those dizzying heights &
        my stanzamina's not what it used to be
I couldn't keep it up for long
    even with a full prescription for Verbiagra

Besides, the show has to end some time
    & you eventually have to put your feats
                on the ground
That's why I prefer to be
        an agrolinguist
        a word horticulturalist
      stay down to earth
        within reach
          deeply rooted in rich soil
  not afraid to get dirty
      plant seeds in your minds
            hearts
            souls
  & watch
      them
          grow.

Foreplay on Words

Last night was amazing
Last night we met at that small café
    proceeding slowly
            cautiously
      like animals abused but
        still willing
          wishing
          needing to be loved
Last night we met at that small café
    meeting there for the first time, as if we were
    meeting there for the first time
      cautious at first with our movements
                our words
                our sharing
        slowly catching up
          reconnecting
          remembering
          rekindling that old flame
            & then the music started
You turned to me & said,
    "Do you still know how to dance?"
I mirrored your face
      your raised eyebrows
      your sly grin
      your flush cheeks
    following your mind down that path

                   innuendos strewn like clothing once was
     I took you in my hand & led you to the floor
     Like all the couples who took center stage before us
            all eyes focused on us
                   curious to hear our song
                          to see our moves
                          to feel our fire
            & we moved like fire across sere forests
                   moved like waters surging over levees
                          like whirlwinds over Kansas
                          like earth dark
                                 damp &
                                 deeply inclined to
                                        separate CA from itself
            we moved like lightning across August skies
                   moved like spirits intertwined thru the ether
                   moved like elementary
                          like experts in dance
                          like animals no longer cautious but
            hungry
            hunting
            hurting for each other's flesh
            thirsting for the refreshment
                   only each other's soul can give
     we moved like lovers on display
            like live pornography
            like an orgy of words
            sexing each other good
                   while fucking the audience
            mouths agape with
                   all the different meanings of
                          O

When our dance was done
    we left the stage trembling
        for different reasons than when we started
We were polite & waited for others to take their turns
    enjoying their dances but
        all the while knowing that
            soon enough but not
            soon enough
                we could leave
                we could go
                we could be somewhere else
                      be alone somewhere
When the time came
    we lingered behind
        shaking hands
        making plans
        pretending there was no urgency
                    no unspoken agreement,
but
        knowing what was to come
Finally, I was alone with you
    eager to get naked again
        to know each other intimately
        to dance in new ways
The music started again
    just for us this time
        & we start strumming familiar notes
            tracing established lines
            strolling down well-trodden paths
Pardon the pun, but
    it's literally been years

                since anyone's touched me there
                    & made it feel this good
                            so good
                    that we spent all night on foreplay
                forced to put off future exploits
        until another time
& there was another time
& there'll be another time
        for future exploits
                exploration
                experimentation &
                exhibitionism
            behind closed doors &
                for all the world to see
    there'll be another time
            for sharing sweet sensual seduction in speech
            for strewing innuendos & clothing
            for all-night foreplay on words
        & for dancing naked to the music we make.

Close Analysis

So, you were right
I couldn't hold on
   couldn't hold on to paradise
     without picking at it
          picking it apart
          putting it under a microscope
       & nothing holds up under that level of scrutiny
But before you start all the finger-pointing
                   tongue-lashing
                   blame-laying
   maybe you should take off those
      rose-colored glasses &
         see your angel as fallen as she is
             as we all are
         with her molting wings
             her broken, tarnished halo in hand
Perhaps you should take another look at her paradise &
   see the weeds in her garden
      the barren desert areas &
      the muggy, pest-laden swamps
I am thin
   but not as unhealthy as you would like to believe
      & surely, in love, one size does not fit all
Think of this before you blame me
   for not being big enough to wear her jacket

I am traveling to places her vehicle can't go
    & carrying baggage it can't handle
Without your filters, I can see her look & smile
    is of a used-car salesman
        with years in the trade of old love
Her sales pitch is heavy-handed
    & what she's selling is in need of repair
        before it's suitable to drive
There are holes in her story
    some filled with putty &
        covered with paint just a shade off
    others left as gaping as my jaw
It's no wonder I only wanted a test drive
    but pressure led to sale
        & now I'm holding you all to the Lemon Laws
        of the state of Love
But you play lawyers & insurance agents
    looking to avoid your client paying her fair share
        in the violent & untimely death of our love
    looking to lay the blame instead on the patient
Perhaps your nursemaid is no Florence Nightingale
Perhaps she missed the ID bracelet
    mentioning allergies to her type of medicine
Despite her years of practice
    she was like a surgeon cutting for the very first time
        as her favorite artist sings
    she wasn't used to a patient with my type of illness
    she tried transplanting the wrong organ
        didn't match the blood type
Now you expect to hold *me* responsible
    for the rejection?

Mind you, I'm not saying I was faultless
                                        baggage-less
                                        disease-less
        I'm not saying I was an angel
    fallen or otherwise
I was
I *am* just a man
      a man of science
    looking under a microscope
    wondering if the problem wasn't that I looked too closely
        but that no one else looked closely enough.

Where I'm Comin' From

"So, where ya' comin' from?"
      "So, where ya' goin' to from here?"
Seems to be the questions people most often ask travelers:
    where ya' comin' from?
        where ya' goin' to?
I suppose those questions could easily be answered by
    simple mental regurgitation of
        my home state & next destination
            but where's the fun in that?
So!
You wanna know where I'm comin' from
You wanna know where I'm goin' to
                              let me tell ya'

I'm comin' from Eden
I'm comin' from the lost paradise
That's right, I found it
      marked it
      know right where it is
      can go back any time I want
Want me to take you there?
Well, right now you'll have to find it on your own
    'cause I'm movin' forward
            onward
            upward
        no more retracin' my own steps
           resurrectin' the past
          relivin' the pain that it took me
                        to find it

I'm comin' from another galaxy
    not here to save your world
        here to *rock* your world
            & show y'all the power of love & positivity
I *am* faster than a speeding bullet
    more powerful than a locomotive *and*
    able to leap tall buildings in a single bound
                when I want to
Wanna see it?
    Well, you're seein' it!
Couldn't tell?
    Then, you ain't gettin' it yet!
See, this is where I'm comin' from
Over the rainbow &
        under the sea
Over the river &
        through the 'hoods
From down on the corner
    & from another dimension
        another plane of existence
        takin' it to another level
        takin' it to the streets
I'm comin' from out'cho closet
    not like a drag queen, honey
        like your best & worst dream
        like a skeleton dancin'
        like a bogey man
        like Da' Boogie Man, standing strong
            lettin' y'all know
                you *will get off me!*
                    & in return, I will get you off!

Folks,
    I'm comin' straight from the heart &
       shootin' straight from the hip
  I'm comin' from a magical place
     where peace & tranquility
        can mean serene silence or
            celebratory screams
  I'm comin' from the place where chaos
     comes full circle
     turns to stillness
  I'm comin' from a place
    where ain't nobody cryin'
      ain't nobody worryin', no
  I'm comin' from a place deep within my soul
       a place that makes where I'm
     goin'
    truly
   anywhere I want to be
It's my own personal, portable Neverland
   & I'd show you how to get there
     but I think you always knew the way
      second star to the right
       & straight on
         to a brand new mornin'
           c'mon, now ...
I'll take you there ...

O Brother, Where Art Thou?

We once lived in the same city
    but for almost 15 years, we never knew each other
When we finally met
    we were brothers
        kindred spirits
            soul mates living in each others' hearts
    & we lived comfortably there for another 15 years
        close like neighbors
    even when the whole country came between us
But something happened to send you back home
    & the closer you came
        the more distant you became
            until you were barely reachable
Now, we again live in the same city
    & I'm feeling again like we don't know each other
For all I know, we could be next-door neighbors
    facing the same fence from different sides
        but reaching out to you
            would still stretch me too far
You're a mystery to me
    your land a dark lot to my soul
I'm afraid of what guard dogs may bite
    should I cross property lines
        of what home fires may burn
    should I dare to reach out my hand

I can't even ask you to reach out to me
    without you snipping like I'm a hedge
        blaming me for growing
    what poison you planted
      when I'm already too short
          from other people's cuts at me
      to stand any of yours
I can't reach out to you
    & I can't ask you to reach out to me
I'm left with no option but to assume
          to act as if
        to believe
    that you're not really there for me anymore
We again live in the same city
    but after almost 35 years,
      we never really knew each other
        did we?

Change Now like Never Before

So, you say O can't fulfill his promises for change
He just keeps giving you the same ol' same ol'
You say you "want change now like never before"
    because you never wanted change before
The same ol' same ol' was good enough for you before
    when a different letter ruled the roost
You were content to watch W bet the farm
      & then watch it be foreclosed on
You backed a war against a scapegoat
    but don't back one against
        people who actually attacked us
You gave W eight years to make this mess
    but don't even want to give O one to fix it
How can you blame O for making back-door deals
    when your people block the front?
How can you cut off his legs & then
    blame him for crawling?
How can you stop him from acting right
    & then blame him for acting wrong?
How can you blame him for doing
    what politicians do,
        when your picks do it, too
        when they make it impossible
           to do anything else
           to *be* anything else besides
        a politician?

He's just playin' the game
        playin' the polls
        playin' the people as best as he can
     given the circumstances
But you're suddenly tired of the game
                tired of being played
                      tired of the same ol' BS from BHO
You feel betrayed by Mr. Change We Can Believe In
    & suddenly you want change now
                                like never before
    so, when the last lion dies by black magic dagger
        carving up his cerebrum with a capital C
    you don't seek a sit-in but a full-on replacement
        because you want change now
                              like never before

And your choice is?
Well, we could call him SB
    but it's the same ol' BS
        the same ol' same ol'
    that got us into this mess
News flash:
Change ain't comin' through that door
Just get more & more of the same
    power-hungry whore like before
A revolving door spinning you dizzy
    pushing it 'til you're sore, loser
You're a sore loser
    but we all are
        we've all lost
        we're all lost
        we all lost our way from what we really need

'Cause what we really need
    Is **real** change
Not the change we can fall for
    the changing into one of two shirts
        not making sure if either is clean
But the change we can **really** believe in
    changing into a new outfit
        a new wardrobe
        a new style
        a new way of doing things
            of seeing things
            of seeing ourselves
Goin' out for a night on the town with our girl America
    &, instead of just bouncing back & forth between
        two lame parties
    we take it to a whole other club
        & get things really movin'
See, as long as the guards don't change
    then there's no point in the changing of the guard
        & the only way anyone will learn
        & the only way everyone can grow
    is if we learn to pick "other"
        the only way we can see real change
    is if we learn to pick each other
        learn to pick each other up
            not pick **at** each other
            but pick **for** each other's good
    not just our own
You talk about how your home's got you covered

so you shouldn't have to worry about
     the rest of the nation's coverage
but it's time to start covering each other
     rather than covering up mistakes
          time to start opening hearts & minds
     instead of closing ranks
  & it's time to change the system
     rather than just changing parties
               just changing parties?
That's not the kind of change you can believe in
That's just the kind of change that,
     the more it changes,
          the more it stays the same
So, if you **truly** want change now like never before
     you need to change yourself
               change the way you think
                    the way you speak
                    the way you act
     you need to **be** the change you seek
          & then look within to find it
Only then can you encourage it in others
If you want change now like never before
     then **change** now like never before
     then change things now
          to be something like never before
Not like they are now
          or were then
Like
Never
Before.

That Guy in That Picture

I'm hoping to get laid tonight
I'm looking around the room & thinking
    I'm hoping to get laid tonight
I'm looking around the room
     & seeing plenty of pleasing prospects
    my level
    eye level
    thigh level
      thin & frail &
      the orca whale
    I'm just hoping to get laid tonight
Taking in the sights like taking inventory
            like picking pets out of the pen
            like picking produce
   squeezing ripe melons
     no, not that one
        that one &
        that one &
          that one
Her
    her
        her &
          him
    I'm just hoping to get laid tonight
Now, I write
   & recite
      about love in full flight

        about equal rights
        about wars & fights
          & other blights
        about dawn's early light
            afternoon delight
                twilight &
          midnight moonlight
I write about all the ways to treat a lover right, but
    I'm just hoping to get laid tonight
I write about issues that are important to women
                important to people
                important to life
    & I'm hoping to get laid tonight
I write about issues that are important
    & I'm hoping to get laid tonight
These statements don't have to be incongruous
                      inconsistent
                      incompatible
                        with each other
    nor does it have to mean
        that I'm doing the first
            just to get the second
It doesn't have to mean
    that I don't mean what I say
    that I'm insincere in any way
    that I don't love
        respect
        honor you as a person

It just means that I want sex
                like sex
              love sex
              need sex
              need to feel skin on skin
                    to feel sweet sweaty sin
                to feel you coming
                      again & again
    as I wipe your juice of my chin
                          & grin
Yeah, I'm hoping to get laid tonight
    but that doesn't make my poetry into
                either hypocrisy
                    or conspiracy
It just makes me a man
    not just for loving it
        but for admitting it
Hiding behind the veil of anonymity
    you speak your comments
        like there's something wrong with me
        like there's nothing wrong with you
        like there's not the same thing wrong with you
        like you don't hope
        like no one else hopes to get laid tonight
            or ever
You place your labels
    like you're so much better than me
I just wanted to let you know
    you're not

    not any better than me
        or than that guy in that picture
   to whom you've given my name
But that guy's not me
   never was & never will be
     I am not the me you see
       all poignant poetry
         in a conspiracy of hypocrisy
No, that guy's not me
   doesn't even look like me
     his hair's not as curly
     my goatee's not as wispy
       & I'm more likely to take off my clothes
       than to keep on my coat
        or to hide behind masks like he does
        or   like you do
Perhaps you should take off your veil of anonymity
        let us know who you are
        let us see who looks in the mirror
   & calls his reflection by my name
Perhaps you should take off your blinders &
       let yourself see
   that guy in that picture
    is a reflection
   that guy in that picture
    that guy's not me.

All of You

When I told you I wanted all of you,
    I meant everything, every part.
All I got was your body
      & your apologies.
Oh, don't misunderstand me.
When I told you I wanted all of you,
    I did mean your body, in part.
I wanted to taste the sweet poison from your lips
    killing me softly with each kiss
        just as remembering each kiss kills me now
          but in a different way.
I wanted to bury my face in your neck
    inhaling your essence
    imprinting your scent in my brain
            on my skin.
I wanted to gently run my hands
        my kisses
        my tongue
    all over every inch of your body –
        across your neck & over your shoulders,
        caressing your breasts
        rolling each nipple in between my fingers
        planting little angel kisses on your stomach,
        stroking your inner thighs,
        drinking your sweet juices –

I wanted to hold your soft, warm, naked body close to mine,
    so that maybe, if I held you tight enough,
        we'd become one …
    so that maybe, even after you'd gone,
        your presence would linger …
            & it has never left me.
& as I held you in my arms & slowly entered your body,
    I wanted to become lost in your eyes
        & slowly enter your soul.
Yes, when I told you I wanted all of you,
    I did mean your body, in part …
        but only in part.
I also wanted to know your mind
                your innermost thoughts.
I wanted to take hold of your heart
    as you had captured mine
And I wanted to join with your spirit
            intertwine with your soul
        & forever be a part of you
    just as memories of you stay with me.
I wanted you – body, mind, heart & soul.
When I told you I wanted all of you,
    I meant everything, every part.
All I got was your body
    & your apologies.
Now all I have is your silence
    & your absence
        & memories of you.

Changing Seasons

Like Persephone
I leave the spring of our love
In Winter's cold grasp
                She left for Hades
          Underworld king and guard of
              Both heaven and hell
                            I leave for L. A.
                      For eternal damnation
                          Or Elysian fields
            I travel to hell
       Reach for pieces of heaven
            Chase my destiny
Sweet fragrance of skin
Vivid crystal-colored eyes
And petal-soft lips
              I leave behind this
        Sweet, loving angel flower
          As love has just bloomed
                      But will this new love
                  Survive lonely winter cold
                      Or wither and die?
        Ev'ry "I love you"
   Plants a seed under the snow
        Waits for my return

But flowers will bloom
And be picked by different hands
Bring life to new things
        Spring greets its mistress
        On Persephone's return
        Welcoming her home
                But when I come home
            There will be no flowers where
                Once I planted seeds
        To reach my heaven
        I must lose my greatest love
        I must go through hell
For one final night
I lay in my flower's bed
Reap what has been sown
        And forget my trip
        Burn that bridge when I cross it
        For I can't return
            When the morning comes
            The sun will rise on our tears
                And set on our love
        I will leave our love
        Forever frozen in time
        Encased in winter
I will keep this seed
Plant and watch our flower bloom
With each thought of you

House Fire

To call my father a packrat
    would be an understatement
To call his house a pigsty
    an insult to swine
        everywhere
Jugs of cat food for all the strays,
    toolboxes of reds and blues and grays
More tools than Bob Vila
        Norm Abrams
        Tim "The Tool Man" Taylor
      & all of HGTV
    combined
Dozens of curtain rods & venetian blinds
He can't leave a thing behind
So many bolts, it's ... well ... nuts!
Papers in pillars & piles
Boxes upon boxes of unopened boxes
    of tools, toys, trinkets &
        what does one heterosexual man need
          with so many pairs of pantyhose?
Grit, grease & grime built up over time
    turns orange stove-top
        black as coal
            as a soul grown old
                alone &
                out of date

            like the clothes that block my path
                as doorjambs double as closets
                    cluttered with covered clothes hangers
                as couches become bureaus
                                beds
                                breakfast nooks
In fact, the couch is the place to consume all meals
        homemade or microwaved
            as the radiation from a different box
                cooks this couch potato
Indeed, had his health been in a condition
        capable of continuing this lifestyle,
            living this way
                would make anyone's fortitude fade away
But from fighting the fires atop houses
    or at the end of his cigarettes years ago
        or in the core of his being
    from buying & bingeing on booze
            burning holes in livers, stomachs, hearts & souls
    my father's had one foot in the grave for years
now,
& having the other on a peel
                a package
                a pile of papers
    or any of the other garbage
            which eclipses the view of his floor
    is becoming more hazardous to his health
            every day
He wants
    needs to start anew
        but feels the need to clean up this house
                before he cleans up his act

                    the need to clean up this mess of his life
                        before he leaves it behind
            but sometimes ...
Sometimes, more often than not,
        he can still feel the fire burning inside him
                like a moth follows the flickering flame
                    to find a feasible solution
                    to find possible salvation
Y'see, his job taught him everything there is to know
about fire
        including how to set them successfully
            leaving no evidence behind
If he wanted to, my father could set this place ablaze
        & no one would know it wasn't an accident ...
            so why doesn't he?
Why continue cleaning
        continue clinging onto a junkyard
                            a place anyone else
            would've abandoned by now?
Even in Hell, Hope springs eternal
For the mind slips at times too easily
        & gambling gains go forgotten in secret gardens
            little green clovers sprout up from cracks
Hopes of finding hidden fortunes a stroke of luck
                            a wish come true
That is why he continues serving
    this self-imposed sentence
        in a jail cell with the door wide open
He tells me this, &
    without thinking, words jump from the ledge of lips
                    attempt suicide
        instead slaying their speaker

I say to him, "Dad,
    maybe when your life is this much of a mess,
        sometimes it's better to leave it all behind &
    start over,
            even if it means losing something good."
I didn't even think.
I just said it
    & stopped
      stood still
        struck deaf & dumbfounded
    by my statement's bellowing echoes
        bouncing off the walls of my soul
                of my circumstances
                of my similar situation
I am a beggar
    shacked up in the shell of a corroded house I call
      my life
    which looks almost livable from the outside
        but through the windows of my eyes
            you can see the torment destroying me
                    devouring me
          from the inside outward
This place should've been condemned years ago
                abandoned completely
I shouldn't be here trying to restore it
    but rather rebuilding something new
                somewhere else
The fire inside *my* soul could set this house
                set this *world* on fire
    sending flames soaring to the sky
      & no one would *care*

                if it was an accident or not
            rather revel in the heat & brilliant spectacle
                    of my fireworks
            revolve their worlds around my star
But I have just found my own special secret garden
        a single flower blooming
            in an otherwise barren land
I have discovered priceless treasure
        in ruby lips & crystal eyes
            & a chest holding a heart of gold
My life has become my prison
Her love makes me not want to escape
& an otherwise dilapidated domicile
        becomes a home
                a palace worthy of kings
            from the magic of her smile
                the comfort of her touch
                the sweet fragrance of her
Burning this building would bury my precious flower
        & leave this lot for someone else to build on
I've already spotted a vulture or two
        circling the remains
            black magpies
                with an eye for treasure sparkling
I don't want to let go
        of the most precious thing I've ever known
            but my house grows weaker every day
            & soon there'll be nothing left
                leaving me living in my garden
                homeless, save the shelter of my flower's petals
& we couldn't stand being left open to the elements
It would just kill us both

She knows this & opens the gate to my cell
    beckoning this bird to fly
              to touch the sky
              to leave behind our love
   sacrificed for the sake of saving a dying dream
It starts with a single stroke
        a strike of a match lit long ago
Now the fire of my dreams cannot be contained
The pain burns hotter than my soul
    leaves scars that will not heal
       but the forceful flow of water from our eyes
          can never be enough to quench this flame
I kiss soft ruby lips goodbye
    & let this fire rocket me to the heavens
       & I *am* the star I always dreamed I could
                knew I would become
      showing all my brilliance to the world
But the searing heat of my life's passion
    engulfs this old house
        leaving nothing behind but ashen memory
         sending smoke spiraling skyward
      creating dark clouds overhead
       blocking out my sun
I will never reveal this dark side of my new world
    which will forever be eclipsed
        shadowed by memories
    of a run-down house
      which a special love, somehow
      made home.

A Little Sick
[with apologies to Taylor Mali]

You'll have to forgive me; I'm a little sick
I'm getting over a touch of bronchitis,
    brought on by a raging sinusitis,
        & I feel a bit of laryngitis
            slowly creeping in
A chronic case of halitosis
    has given me a severe neurosis,
        & through osmosis, others' psychoses
            seeped in to my skin, so
You'll have to forgive me; I'm a little sick
Sick of listening to people content to complain,
    of how they forget how to drive in the rain,
        & does anyone signal when changing lanes?
            No wonder road rage exists!
& *there's* another thing I don't get:
    why is it that, when something makes them upset,
        people can't settle things without the threat
            of gunfire, stabbings or fists?
You'll have to forgive me; I'm a little sick
Sick of the boring, the bored & the plain
    sick of the humdrum & the mundane
        sick of the media poisoning my brain
            with its nonsense, drivel & trash
Sick that the food by which man survives,
    the clothes that he wears & the car that he drives ,

nearly every aspect of our lives
    is dictated by those with the cash
I'm sick of hearing about people dying
    from AIDS, cancer or bullets flying
        I'm sick of politicians lying
            to our face; it's so outrageous!
I'm sick from the smog that chokes the trees,
    sick from the oil that slicks the seas,
        sick from the ills of society
            so dangerously contagious
Sick of being subjected to racism
    sexism, heterosexism, ageism
        sick of any word ending in –ism!
            Prejudice should be a crime!
I'm sick of innocents being slain
    sick of the fighting, sick of the pain
        sick in the head from a world gone insane
            & I'm sick of making things r-
                resemble each other audibly
I'm more than just a little sick
    & I don't give a fuck if you forgive me
I'm sick to death of all the premature deaths
    from the ethnic cleansings in eastern Europe
        to the hospitals & clinics in Africa
    from the streets of south-central LA
        to the Midwest high schools
            & we're idly sitting by
                while watching others die
                while letting each other die
                    letting ourselves die
                        compassion die
                        respect die

                        the earth die
Can't you see it dying?
Ebola, AIDS & cancer are *our* diseases
    but they are the *world's* white blood cells
        purging itself of the virus homo sapiens
Every tornado is a cough
Every hurricane a sneeze
Every heatwave a hot flash
Every draught a raging fever
Every earthquake a shiver
Every thunderstorm acid tears fall from the sky
    as the earth cries, "**Help me!**
        Please
            help me."
The earth is sick
    & I'm dying for an extra-strength dose
        of compassion.

Cat & Mouse

In the dream, I am show cat
     strutting & fretting my hour upon cat show stage
         prideful paws prancing & dancing
   as gushers gaze gleefully at my gait
                   my coat
                   my eyes
     delivering news of ribbon blues to front step
In the dream, I am circus cat
   spotlight special in center ring
      tough tiger tamed twirling on tiptoes
        tricks for treats
     taking bows for jumping through hoops on command

In life, dreams become real
   and I *am* center stage spotlight shining
      showing all that I am
        all that I can do
      taking treats of applause and O's standing
   cerebral sponge soaking in the life-sustaining water
     of warm memories
coming house – not home
     to family asking
        telling
        ordering
        begging me to get a "real" job
          when I feel so much closer
             to reaching lifelong goals

In the dream, I am tomcat
                housecat
              companion cat
     occasionally aloof
                alone & independent when I want
                    coming home when I want
                      sleeping when I want
                  doing what I want when I want
         but there when you need me
              cuddling comforting curling up in lap
              listening intently to dreams

In life, I find someone I want to follow home
     but she feels uncomfortable with the title "master"
          tells me I am not strong enough for her
          tells me I am too clingy
                too needy
          tries to send me to a "no-kill" shelter
  failing to realize I'm dead already
      from her words
          "not strong enough"
            not strong enough?
        not given the chance to show my strength
I can see, in my heart, I am strength personified
I can see, in my dreams, I am jungle cat
    black panther stalking
    king lion hunting
    lightning-quick cheetah running
        lean, mean, muscular, majestic, malevolent
            almighty Maker's masterpiece

In the dream, I am alley cat
    streetwise, tough, attitude with fur
    reflexes react exact
        counterattacked with wit sharp as claws
            with fangs of biting sarcasm
            with words as other weapons
            with physical &
                mental prowess

In life, I stand in the street
    ready to defend my turf
            my friends
            my life
    instead waiting,
        supposedly
    for the safety in numbers
    against one
    instead wondering what everyone else sees
        that I can't

In the dream, I am cat
    lean, mean, muscular, majestic, malevolent,
        mystical
            almighty Maker's masterpiece

In life, I sit in front of the TV
    watching antics of cartoon high jinks
        wondering if Jerry, too, was a cat in his dreams.

Hurricane Nici

There is a fine line
    between the beauty
        the freedom
        the nakedness
           of not having your own boundaries
    & the clumsy
        thoughtless
        graceless
        butchery
           in failing to respect someone else's
You dance on that line like a ...
                well ...
When one normally draws comparison
    between dancer & animal
        the first that comes to mind is a gazelle
    but watching you dance on that line
        brings other African animals to mind
A charging rhino
Stampeding wildebeest
A ballerina elephant
    with a mouse for a partner
Now, I'm not trying to make any weight jokes
    because I think everyone knows
        that's never been important to me
& I'm not trying to say you don't move gracefully
                because you do
        or you're not beautiful
                because you are

so I guess it's a bad way to describe
    how you tread
  or how you *shred*
      the fine line between *care-free*
                & *careless*
Instead, I'll say
   you are a butterfly
     vibrant & beautiful
     flitting between African flowers
  while I stand on American shores
    & watch my house fall apart
       in the winds of your hurricane love.

Sexual

Bigots blind themselves from the truth
    with what they believe to be true
        & even the open traps of open minds
            cannot capture the concept
            cannot conceive of reality
The debate rages on
    like the river of blood rushing through my veins
        carrying the cryptic code we debate
            & the hormones at the heart of the matter
But debaters are still baffled
                bewildered
                blinded to the truth their eyes see
But if they
    if we
        were blinded
        wore blindfolds
            we would see
Let our other senses take over
                talk to us
                tell us the truth
Listen to hear heartbeats & heavy breathing
Smell the scent of sweat & pheromones
Taste tender kisses from an unknown tongue
Feel that tongue & hands & skin on skin
    all over your body

    all over your body
          your body
            is
               sexual
Not hetero-
Not homo-
Not a- or bi-
Just
    sexual

The debate is over.

Farewell to Fairy Fantasy

Something came alive in me today
    when I saw you, sweet fairy princess
        flaming hair
        flowing dress
        floating in
Flawless beauty
Goddess incarnate
Love personified
    & my heart soared when you entered the room
            sang in every embrace
            sighed at every smile
                & every spoken word
        & I knew love
            felt love
            dreamed of love eternal
                    of days filled with laughter
                    of nights filled with pleasure
                    of dawns waking to your face
                            your voice
                            your touch
            starting the cycle anew
Something died in me today
    when I saw you, sweet fairy princess
    when I saw the sadness in your eyes
    when I heard the words you spoke
                    you spoke spears striking
        into the flesh of my dream

You spoke of your dream image
           your mirror self-smashed
Your love denied you
    taking with him pieces of you
           pieces you now
      can never again share
           pieces I now
      can never really know
Now I see my dream for what it is
    just a dream to hold a fairy
           such folly finally
        set free
I cannot keep a dead dream
    for it would drain me
      'til I died, as well
So I close my eyes
    & I see you, sweet fairy princess
      flaming hair
      flowing dress
      face in my hands
Slowly, I kiss soft lips goodbye
    cut my cord from dreams that die
      & let me set free
        a fairy
           to fly.

Grow Up

A junior high school student can learn words like
    fornication
    copulation
    reproduction
        & have all the necessary parts in working order
but that doesn't make one grown-up enough
        to actually do it
            & accept the consequences
    yet hundreds
        thousands do it everyday
& we scold
    lecture
    admonish them
    & mourn the loss of their innocence
& we do what we can to prevent others
    from following in their footsteps
        falling into their fate
        because we know that
            for all their knowledge
        they're just not ready
                to be that grown-up yet
So, too, have you fashioned yourself a grown-up
    with your big, fancy words
        & your grown-up worries
You have a husband
        a house
        a hat-trick of tykes

      two incomes
      two cars
      too much debt
So, too, have you fashioned yourself a grown-up
    with your grown-up worries
        & your big, fancy words
    but a rose by any other name would smell as sweet
        & the fertilizer you're shovelin' is still …
See, when you were little
    using words like "prevaricator"
        would get you a gold star on a spelling test
            applause at a spelling bee
            a lot of positive attention
    but now
        it'll just get you slapped
A polysyllabic insult
    is still an insult
& what you're doing to my head
        my heart
        my life
    is the same damn things
      you've always done
    for the same damn reasons
      you've always done them
Your new methods of doing them
    are like calling it fornicating with me
Sure, it sounds big & fancy
    but it doesn't make you a grown-up.

Blue

What is the color of empty?
I know the color of nothing
But I don't feel like nothing
I feel like something
          something
                    empty
As I stand here alone with you
As I stand her with you
                    alone
I see a roomful of people
I see a roomful of empty
Fill me up
Fill up my container with what I need
            or with what I'm looking for
   they're not necessarily the same thing
Make me full with the something I'm missing
Let me fill you with me
I'm tired of being full of shit
I'm tired of being full of empty
I long for the warmth of your full
   as I stand in the cold of my empty
& this cold cannot be shaken with cloth
                    with coat or blanket
   for it comes from my empty
     which comes from within
         & chills me **from** the bone to the skin
           turning me to ice
           turning me blue
What is the color of empty?
The color of empty
                    is me.

These Old Papers

Should I bother to keep these old papers?
There are scribblings on them
        words of some sort
        words of mine,
                I guess
I mean, it's my handwriting,
    so I assume it's American English
        but I look at them now
           & can't decipher a single thing
What ancient & foreign language is this?
    Sanskrit?
    Hieroglyphics?
    Esperanto?
It's all Greek to me
Perhaps, if I read with my eyes
    my brain could process all the information
        but that won't help the cause
           won't answer the question
No, to see the worth of these words
    you must know their true meaning
        to know the true meaning of these words
    you must feel it
        to feel the true meaning of these words
    you must read with your heart
If I truly put the words on these old papers
    that should be easy for me

        but it hasn't been, so far
            & it's not looking good
I'm calling the past for inspiration
      but the number is as disconnected from this as I am
          can't get the feelings on the lines
It's just not clicking for me
     well, not the way that I want
         more like the click you hear
            before the dial tone
Maybe I should conduct a séance
              call up these ghosts to haunt
     the spaces left in my heart
            receive the messages from the spirits
     that fill the blanks on these old papers
     that make them worth something again
         but the spirits behind these pieces stay silent
Where's Jon Edwards when you need him?
Oh, well.
Maybe it's best if the electric spark of inspiration
     has left this body of work
I'm no Dr. Frankenstein
     to resurrect the dead with lightning
         for the monsters created could be far worse
Better to give these words the burial they deserve
     bodies crumpled together
          dumped into the paupers' mass grave
     called waste basket
I need to let go
       to leave the past behind
       to move on to the new
            the now

I need to focus on today
I need to give these words back
    to the person who really wrote them
      the me lost in the ether
        with a thousand yesterdays
I need to forget what I can't remember
I need to
I *want* to just answer the question
No.
No, I don't need to keep these old papers
        these old rusted thoughts
        these feelings forever unfinished
No
    & that one word overpowers all the others
    & the papers crumple underneath its weight
    & with them, shackles to the past
      fall away into the waste basket
        finally left behind.

Tattooed

My trademark cursive j.
    adorns her wrist like it was born there
        a brand worn with pride
            worn for all to see
She joked once that, if we broke up
    it would tell her exactly where to put the razor
It takes no effort to hold back a laugh that's not there
It takes too much to hold back a love that is
Brands are meant to mark roaming cattle
    but it is the herder that has
        moved on to other pastures
            though not necessarily greener
In fact, lately it's been a bit barren but
    that's okay
I didn't come here running *toward* something
I came here running *away*
    for *she* wore the brand but *I* was the cattle
        young veal kept in the cage she made
        forced into roles I wasn't ready to play
            but I tried to be her puppet
                because she pulled on my heartstrings
Eventually I became her Pinocchio
        did her dance
    without her controlling the steps
        but no matter how hard I tried
            I couldn't keep my nose from growing

Part of me never felt comfortable living with this lie
This isn't working
    this dance
I'm tripping too much over legs too often unused
This head of cattle was meant to roam free ...
    although, when the cage was open,
        I gawked for a minute
            unsure of what to do
                how to move
            where to go
I didn't know any other life than this
    & there were times of bliss enough
        to tempt me to stay
        but I needed to stray
            to stretch my legs & run away
        but not from her
            from the me she wanted me to be
          because it wasn't me
        so now I'm free
           to search this barren wasteland
              for the sustenance that I am
            search for what I am
          without her attached to me
        like my trademark cursive j.
    is attached to her wrist
She joked once that, if we broke up
    it would tell her exactly where to put the razor
It takes no effort to hold back a laugh that's not there
It takes too much to hold back a love that is
In my time with her
    I grew to love her

  grew to know her love until
    it all became second nature
She used to be attached to me
  like my trademark cursive j.
   is attached to her wrist
Now, it takes too much effort to hold back
  the "I love you"
    tattooed to the roof of my mouth
     where she no longer goes.

So What?

The Goddess stands naked in the Temple to the Word
    beckoning others to join her in nakedness
The Priestess stands naked in the Temple to the Word
    as parishioners pray to her
        almost as much as the Muses
The Hostess stands naked in the Temple to the Word
    singing her seductive siren song
      luring lovers to lingering death
        sweet smiles on their faces
          as they watch the Temple crumble, as well
The Empress stands naked in the Temple to the Word
    & speaks the spell that makes its walls
        tumble & decay
          while parishioners still pack hallowed
                    hollowed halls
            praying to Priestess posed &
              reposed
            praying to image of Goddess
              gone long ago
                from the Temple to the Word
No one heard the voice of the little boy
    among the throng of worshippers
No one heard him exclaim
    not that the Empress had no clothes
      but that she still wore a mask
          still hid her face

behind a façade of fake flowers
    still hid scars & blemishes &
other imperfections like ours
    still hid eyes
boarded windows to an empty soul
    still hid motives &
        methods of
        madness
    behind a mask
No one heard our half-pint hero herald
    that the Goddess was never completely naked,
        after all
Well, *some* heard
    but it reached their ears like
        "wolf," cried too many times
Besides, our clever Goddess
    had prepared her people from day one
        with a mantra stolen from the lips of *her* God
        a mantra made meaningless
            for many moons
        through constant repetition &
            association
        with its false Goddess
So, no one noticed that the Empress
    was never really naked
& no one noticed that she
    was never really ruler of anything
And no one noticed
    for nearly a decade
        that the walls of the Temple decayed
            until nothing was left but the memory

Some even blamed the boy
      for waking them from dreams of yesteryear
Some sent him running away
      not to return 'til he was all grown up
            ... well, for the most part, anyway
                  but this isn't for them
It's not for bleary-eyed sheeple
      alarmed to waking without coffee
It's not for the scapegoat kid
      suffering sleepy sheeple bleating
                  like a beating
                        'til bleeding before
                      beating it
It's not even for false Goddess
      of whom, I'm told,
            we can still gleam glimpses occasionally
No, this is for the men of La Mantra
      who remember its true meaning
            & build a new house of worship
                  a new Temple to the Word
            not on images of false idols
                  but a much stronger foundation.

Your Name in My Mouth

Your name in my mouth
    feels like home
    feels like ohm
        resonating on the universal frequency
        at once calming & energizing me
            putting me in tune with the muse
                in tune with the world
                      with the universe
                          the All
                      with myself
                                with you
Your name in my mouth
    is music
    is meditation
    is my way of praying
            of saying everything that matters
Your name in my mouth
    is a home-cooked meal
        mouth-watering
        lip-smacking
        rib-sticking goodness
            at once filling me to stuffed
                & leaving me starving for more
Your name in my mouth
    is a magic spell of immeasurable power
        creating & destroying & creating new worlds

    hypnotizing all who hear it in my head
            in my heart
            in my soul
   setting aflame spirits
   giving wings to angels
     like ringing a bell
        a chime in tune with <u>ohm</u>_____
It is at once sweet & sour
  tangy candy
  nectar of the Gods
        on my tongue
I want to show you how that feels
      how that sounds
      how that tastes
        on my tongue
I want you to know what it is for me
  to have your name in my mouth

Come closer.

Color Blind

Life is not in shades of gray
    not always, anyway
See, you can't make gray
    without adding black to white
        or vice versa
        which means black & white have to at least
        exist
The black & white exist
    out in life somewhere &
        eventually, you'll encounter them
Eventually, you'll encounter the moments when
    something's just not right <u>*at all*</u>
        not <u>*one single bit*</u>
    or the moments that make you write
        about perfect moments, to
            freeze them in time, like a pristine winter
    & not every winter day snows
Sometimes, not one speck of white
    will hit the blackest night
        & sometimes no volcanic ash
            falls on the white mountainside
Life is not in shades of gray
    not always, anyway
Sometimes, life is not black & white
Sometimes, life is the yellow of chicken skin
    hiding behind anonymity
        behind the Internet
        or behind excuses
Sometimes, life is a red haze over eyes

world on fire to burn it down with your rage or
red from tears, as a red heart tears or
hazing blurry from altered states
        altered minds
        altered realities
    or realities left behind
Sometimes, it's green with envy
        green with illness
        green with death
        green with life anew
No, the world is too full of colors
    to be limited to just shades of gray
Every color gets its day
        its hour
        its season
        its time
A story has two sides
    but so does a dime
        & the chances of flipping it & landing on its side
        are astronomical
The inverse can be said of flipping a story
    & landing on the truth
A story has two sides & the truth
    usually falls somewhere in between, but
  it *usually* falls somewhere in between
Sometimes, it falls on one side or the other
    shining silver in your eye, &
Sometimes, the story's a die
    white cube
    black pips
    six sides
        & no gray

Sometimes, it's got twenty sides numbered
    & comes in an array of color options
Take a roll
Take a chance
Take a guess as to where it will land &
        as to whether it will land
          on its edge
    even less likely
See, life just doesn't work that way
You can't always guess how the die's gonna lay
    & you won't always see life
        in shades of gray
Sometimes, you have to pick your color
                your number
                your card
                your side
      so make sure you see with open
Try to not be color blind
See things as they are
    not the grays you may want them to be
    not whatever makes life easy
        but as they truly are
    especially on the days
        when it *does* come up gray
Even gray has its day in the sun
    some shade or another in view
        with enough light on the subject
            hopefully
        to be able to tell
So, can you tell
    or are you still seeing things
        through gray-colored glasses

             clinging to neutrality so hard
        you can't see the beauty in the contrast?
May as well have blinders on, too
    obscuring your peripherals
        only seeing in front of you
        only seeing forwards
        not seeing that you're being led
            in circles
                like a comet, drawn to a star
            that doesn't even think of you
                as part of her system
            your dirty gray ice mist tail trailing
                dirty gray ice fog clouding your view
Let go
Let go of your orbit & pick a place to crash land
    take a stand
    take a side of a planet
        solidly grounded or rogue
        light side or dark side
            but pick a side
                before your star goes nova
                        goes nowhere
              like a Nova in Mexico
Just get behind the wheel
Take control
                & get on the right side of the road
That is,
    provided you can tell the yellow lines
        from the white.

Education & Experience

I

Your green dress
    looks horrible
        on me
First, it's not the right shade of green
    to go with my complexion
        & it doesn't bring out my eyes
Also, it's too big in the shoulders
    too wide in the hips
    too short in the skirt
          & it's a *dress*
            & I'm a *guy*

Granted, I'm bi
    but I'm not a transvestite!
Still, if I were,
    that green dress wouldn't work for me
        the way it works for you
        the way it fits your curves
           goes with your complexion
        & brings out your eyes.

II

The Last Seduction, starring Linda Fiorentino,
    is a good movie
I see that now, after years of studying & producing films

I did not have the benefit
    of my education & experience
        when I first watched the film
  did not know what to look for
    that would make a movie good
All I knew was that I was hooked
  right from the beginning
  right until the ending
    which was such a shock to my system
            to my senses
            to my sense of
                right & wrong
    that I wanted my money back
      & I saw it for free
But I wanted more than a refund of unspent money
    I wanted to get back the time I wasted
                time I lost
    wanted to *give* back the memory of this movie
    wanted to free the space it occupied in my brain
      without giving the good payoff
                the filthy squatter
Only in becoming more educated & experienced
    had I realized the rent *had* been paid.

III

A friend once told me that karma is like shopping:
  some people pay with credit &
    get the good stuff now
  but they'll have to pay the bill later
      & it's usually for more than the stuff is worth;

others have to work harder & longer
       to pay cash up front
    but when you get the good stuff, it's *yours*
      you own it forever &
          no one can take it away
     which makes it worth more
I'm trying to learn how to make only cash payments
  & how to accept all major credit cards
    how to let other people's eventual payment plan
      be the Great Banker's problem
        & not mine

IV

I've had many a teacher try to give me lessons
  on how to be a good lover
        a good partner
        a good friend
        a good son
        a good parent
        a good adult
        a good man
        a good person
Some classes were private tutoring;
  others were massive lecture halls
Some lessons were elementary;
  others were on a collegiate level so advanced,
    I'm not even sure the *teacher* could always follow it
Some teachers had *earned multiple* degrees;

    others were only honorary,
        while others barely had an associate's
Never before, though,
   have I ever wanted a tuition refund
      as badly as I do from you
I don't know what course
    the Great Administrator assigned you to teach
      but I feel like I learned nothing
              I gained no new knowledge
            earned no certificate
             didn't even get to cross the stage
     I got nothing positive out of this
& it makes me want to get back the time I wasted
                        time I lost
                              on you

   makes me want to *give* back the memory of us
              to free the space it occupies
          in my brain
makes me want to forget
   how good you looked in that green dress
   how I helped you pick it out in the store
   how I showed you off to your friends
     & everything that came before it
     & everything that came *after* it
But sometimes people pay with credit
   & sometimes managers misplace receipts
I can only hope that Dr. Time

will give me enough education & experience
   to know where to look.

The Good Fight

It took some time
    & a lot more thought than you're worth
        but I think I can finally explain
            the knife you said was in your back:
It was thrust there by your own hand
            your own need
    to perpetuate drama
        that was no longer there
The reason it has my prints on it
    is because I handed it back to you
        hilt first
        after you had thrust it in mine
I tried to bring down a kingdom that stood against you
The least you could've done
    was given me stable ground on which to stand
        not pull the rug out from under me
            setting up the situation
                so that you could then
                    fall on your sword
        which you didn't even bother to clean
You found my prints
    but you missed my blood under yours
Now, your efforts to show me what you "found"
        to share your discovery
    only do more damage
You should learn to turn the handle out
    when flashing your blade
        like I did, when I gave it back to you

You should learn to handle your weapons properly
     not fall on them & blame innocent bystanders
         for your mess
You should learn
             a lot of things
   about fighting
   about friendship
   about fairness
   about life
       but that's the heart of the problem, isn't it?
You talk a good game about fighting the good fight,
    but you don't know anything about it.

Junkie

She tells me that, if I really didn't want it
    I wouldn't have let it happen
& I can't help but wonder
    how those words could escape the same mouth
        whose nos were ignored one night long ago
& I know it's not the same
        not exactly
& I know she didn't attack me with a weapon or a drug
    but she kinda did
See, words are weapons sharper than knives
    & no word was ever sharper than her well-honed
        "oh"
Sharp as a needle through my skin
    she injects lust
        passion
        romance
            into a junkie a few months clean
        places the sample on my tongue
            with her tongue
        & expects me not to suckle at her mouth
            like a starving infant
            begging
            pleading
            screaming for more

I'm a love junkie
    a sex addict
    a horn dog in heat on a hot summer night
        & it's a fight to stay clean
            when my body longs to be dirty
                            sweaty
                            sticky
        because a thick layer of smut
                protects against feeling pain
                      feeling real
                      feeling
                                anything
    anything I don't want to feel
        & I don't want to feel   anything
      not even this lust
        unless I *must*
        unless I'm moved
                by more than the moon
        unless I'm pulled
                by the gravity of her gaze
            from the stars in her eyes
        unless I'm touching heaven
            & can still stay rooted in earth
        unless I'm sober
                of sound mind
                & clear head
But I'm caught in the haze of this hot summer night
    & the silver sliver looms low & large in the sky
        more accomplice than witness

    watching &, at the same time
    weighing me down
    holding me down
      as romance roofies
         wreak havoc in my head
I can't think straight
  all I can see is this fire &
  all I can hear is this music &
  all I can feel is this heat
     & this haze
     & her hands &
  all I can hear is her moans &
    I lost it
     lost control
    lost sight of my goal
I fell onto her &
  off the wagon as easily as
    clothes fell off our bodies
& then she tells me that, if I really didn't want it
  I wouldn't have let it happen
  I could've said no, &
  I could've said no, but
    when I said, "Whoa" &
      tried to catch my breath
       clear my head
    my word was met
        with her mouth on mine again
    muffling
    muddling
    muting my mind
      like she held the control as
       she held my head in place

                    when all I wanted to do was
                              pause
                              rewind
                            just stop
                    she just wanted to play
                          fast & forward &
forcing
          is too strong a word for
            what happened here
      but catching a cop without Kevlar
             off-duty & off-guard
         doesn't mean he wants to be shot
so, to light a fire
      play soft music
      rub my back &
      moan in my ear
         on a hot summer night
         with the moon hung low
         & my defenses down
      & then tell me some part of me *wanted*
(pardon the pun)
         what came next
            is unfair
         as unfair as it is
             for me to compare
                assaults & violations
             to these tender passions fulfilled
      but my twisted mind & broken heart

         see both sets of scenarios as detrimental
                              dangerous
                              deadly
             if handled improperly
& I wanted so badly to handle this properly
                              tenderly
                              gingerly
     with a delicate touch for this box labeled
          Caution: Contents Fragile
I know she won't be broken as badly by me
      as she was when her last handler dropped her
           but she can still bruise the delicate skin
                of her fruitful heart that I have labeled
                     forbidden
           & she can still damage
                when she should build
           & she can still weaken
                when she should strengthen
           & she can still weep
                     still leak juice that the worthy
                would call ambrosia
                     nectar of the Gods
                but I just call smack
                     crack
                     liquid courage
                     some chemical
                to alter my brain
                     reacting badly, when mixing
                          with the unstable elements
                              burning in my blood

She says I couldn't deny the chemistry
    & I don't deny there's chemistry
        but I don't want that chemical fix
            only to have it blow up in my face
    I'm not willing to settle for chemistry
        when I know how alchemy feels
    I'm not looking to create chemical concoctions
        when I know I can make magic happen
            with the right ingredients
            & time
I want her to find this, too
    because she deserves no less
        but she sees it in me
            when it's not there
        & she wants it in me
            when I don't
        & she pushes it on me
            when there's no pull
                except the pull of hair
                    & the grasp at straws
                    & the feeling dark walls
                        searching for an exit
    but she pushes still &
        pushes harder, hoping I'll
                        fall
                            for her
& I don't want to push back
        push away
      & lose a friend
          a great friend

a like mind
a kindred spirit
but she's not a soul mate
doesn't stir things in my
black cauldron heart
& make magic happen
it's just hormones
chemicals
drugs in my system
she doesn't pull me with the gravity in her gaze
& make my heart fly in space
it just weighs me down
makes me heavy with guilt & sadness
& I don't want to tell her
to risk everything
but I know from too much experience
that hiding the truth
hiding myself
will only make it worse
So, I try to tell her as gently but
as plainly as I can
& she tells me that, if I really didn't want it
I wouldn't have let it happen
I could've said no, but
I couldn't deny the chemistry
& she's right

but we don't always want what's good for us,
do we?

A Haiku Series for a Series of Women

Sonya
10-year-old's first kiss
Discarded for real cooties
Regrets of childhood

Velma/Dena
Best friends for five years;
Lovers should work, almost works;
Years later, nothing

Maura
Alone in the snow
Shoulda, Coulda, Woulda are
My three little words

Kate
Engaged but allowed
To play around with others;
You left when I fell

Yvie
First neutral, then
too/Far too fast; you slow, reverse;
I want out; we stop

Jasmin
Just like "Chasing Amy"
Except where Bob loved her &
Amy was mature

Jamie
Dancer's body with
Angel's voice, dark hair, face
One more love unvoiced

<u>Lori</u>
Your fear killed a love
It was trying to protect
Before it could start

<u>Beth</u>
Finally I'm brave
Enough to say how I feel
& you disappear

<u>Sheila</u>
Resembling a star
Your shine dulled by fear of Dad
Seeing my darkness

<u>Rachel</u>
I saw you first, but
My friends all got their turns in
Before you vanished

<u>"Kristin"</u>
Wildfire hair, spirit
Passion fulfilled; potential
Quickly abandoned

<u>Pamela</u>
Push me where I'm not
Ready to be; drop me when
I start to like it

<u>Jennifer</u>
I liked what I saw
'til the view inside changed with
Your exposed outside

Hannah
My friend became fling
Became more to you than me
I left; you vanished

April
You dreamed small because
You thought it's all you deserved
Trading me for less

Nicole
Too much woman &
Too much little girl, when I
Was not enough man

Christina
I loved the woman
You feigned to be for the man
You tried to make me

Cyndi
I lay with you, then
Lie for you, but for others,
I can't do either

Aletha
You drowned a strong love
In waterfalls of liquor
& oceans of doubt

Heather
A magickal love
Too distant & thrice-tied to
A dangerous man

<u>Meredith</u>
Changing of the guard:
You tired of waiting for me
To just let mine down

<u>Pat</u>
A kindred spirit
But not a soul mate, despite
What our bodies say

<u>Crizzy</u>
Is this not it or
Am I just too broken to
Give as you give me?

<u>The next</u>
Wanted: stoneworker
To turn jaded heart into
Something beautiful

<u>The last</u>
When you're fin'lly here
I hope I can greet you with
Open arms & heart

Words for Luke

One of my greatest fears is to be my father
    leaving this world
    leaving you without
    leaving you anything to build with
                      to build on
        without
    leaving you prepared for battle
                for struggle
                for life
    leaving you *without*
    leaving you lacking
          looking for
          longing for guidance &
          lagging behind
I see you &
I see so much of me in you &
I see so much trouble ahead of you
    so I want to leave you something to
          leave you ready
              ready for the world
I would give you the world, if I could
I would give you everything &
I will give you everything I have, but
        I don't have much to give
        I don't own much &
      what I own
        isn't worth much &
    for what it's worth
      what it's worth
          will go to cover my debts
  & still leave you with a balance
      leaving you   unbalanced
                  unsettled
                unsatisfied &
                insecure

I want to leave you with so much more
    than what I have to give, but
        what I have to give is no more
    than the clothes on my back
      & the words in my heart
           words I never heard from my father

I love you
I love you no matter what &
        no matter what, I will be there for you
    even when I can't
                    be there for you
        I am   there
                          for you
                        with you
                        beside you
                        within you

Remember this
Remember me
Remember the divinity   within you
      the divine light that is you
           that is God within you
Never let anyone dim your light
    for there will be those who try
                try to turn you off
                    turn you down
                    tear you down
                    take you down
                    take pity on them
Remember that haters are just confused admirers
    loving you so much that they want to own you
                      control you
                      contain you
      & they can't

                    unless you let them
                                            don't
                            let them
                        ever
                dim your light
You are more than a bulb to be controlled;
    you are the flash of lightning inside the walls
You are more than a shade to be pulled;
    you are the sun through the window
You are the sun behind clouds
    still shining bright while out of view
Shine on
Burn on
    big &
    bright &
    beautiful
Place clouds where you must
Turn planets when necessary
Choose carefully on whom you shine
            to whom you give your light
                whom you help to grow
    but never stop shining
        even when the world turns its dark side to you
Don't be afraid of the shadows
See them for what they are &
            why they are
                they are only cast there by your light
                    only there
                        to show the difference
Find the beauty in the contrast

    & let it continue to fuel your fire
    &   continue to fuel your fire
        feel it
        feed it
        give it what it needs to keep going
        give you what you need to keep going

                              keep growing
                              keep healthy
                in body & mind
                  & heart & soul
Nothing is more important than your physical
                                    mental
                              & emotional health
                         keep healthy
        give you what you need to keep going
Take time
Make room
Eat right
Work smarter *and* harder
Play the same way
Rest when you need it
Keep your promises
      for your word is all you truly have
Laugh as much as possible
Learn as much as possible
Read as much as possible
Expand your mind
Open   your mind
           your heart
           yourself to the world
Get out & see   the world
         experience the world
         experience life
         experience fear
              feel fear
              feel it
                    but never
                        ever
                            let it hold you back
              feel it
   & then   feel it give way to your will
   & then   feel the rush
                  the high

                    the sense of accomplishment
                            of confidence
                            of completion
            in conquering your fears
                feel that freedom
                    that fullness
                    that feeling &
                every feeling there is to feel
                every feeling
                            including love
                            especially love
                                    love
                                    love others
                                    love yourself
                                    love the world
                                    love life
                                    love strong
                                    love hard
                                    love long &
                                    love true
                                just love
                                    love & be loved
                                        my beloved
                                                son
    as I love you.

More Random Haiku & Senryū

Poets' fluid thoughts
Combine, coagulate, click
Create kick-ass teams

        Hopeless romantic
        Becomes a heartless player
        The music changes

                After her poem
            Some strange force inside urged me
                To use the men's room

    I love all women,
Want to be with every one;
    For that, I am alone

My friends would hit me
If they knew that I was here
Writing more haiku

        Slipping sliding skin
        Soaked in sweat & saliva
        Oh, sweet surrender

                Another for Jasmin
                I know it wasn't
            Love, because I never wrote
                You poetry ... fuck.

        Haiku poetry
Should have to do with nature
        Most of these don't fit

Long for summer heat?
Be careful what you wish for
In the winter winds

        There is no such thing
        As a hopeless romantic
        For love gives all hope

                Your beauty, talent
                Drive & heart inspire me to
                Be awe & dumb struck

        <u>One for Ryk</u>
        What doesn't kill you
        Only doesn't kill you; the
        Rest is up to you

I need more haiku
So that I can fill this page
I don't have enough

        Skipping down the page
        Peeking, looking to find out
        If I filled it yet

                How many is that?
                How many more do I need?
                Am I almost done?

        Even while working,
        Time online can escape you,
        So set an alarm

I want to give you
Poems I will never read
For anyone else

Time Now & Again
[For Lois & Steve]

There's time now
There's time for all the plans we made
    & there's time for making new plans
There's time to see the world on its own turf
                    on our own terms
   & there's time to shut the world out
           shut the world down
           start the world anew
     with you
        you in my world
        you <u>are</u> my world
         & we are in our own little world
                taking on the world &
                taking our time
because we have nothing but time
      & we have everything we need
because we <u>are</u> everything we need
          & everything we ever wanted
    since the beginning of time
    our time beginning now
    our life beginning now
        beginning again
     like the last time &
     like the first time &
          time & time again

>   when we found each other again
>   we have found each other again &
>   we will find each other again
>   time & time again
>   like the first time
>   like the last time
>   like every time
>   at the right time
> How many times could there have been a time
>   & there wasn't a time
>   because it was the wrong time
>   because we didn't have time
>   because we didn't make time
> But now, we've found each other at the right time
>   just in time
>   we've found each other
>   found something in each other
>   found something special
>   something familiar
>   something else
> Now we've got something
> Now we've got everything
> Now we've got nothing but time
>   & we're going to take our time
> So, I want to take this time
>   to promise my time
>   my love
>   myself to you
>   until & beyond the end of time
>   & as time passes,

        I will make the time
        I will take the time
            to keep my promise &
            to show my love
When the time comes
   & the time will come
   as the time is come
   as the time has come
        time & time again
   I will take the time
    to make the time
        to show my promise &
        to keep my love
This time is our time
         & our time has come
Now we have everything
Now we have nothing but
                time.

www.ingramcontent.com/pod-product-compliance
Lightning Source LLC
Chambersburg PA
CBHW052102110526
44591CB00013B/2318